rainbows

What was it like Before Cars?

Paul Humphrey and Alex Ramsay

Illustrated by
Carolyn Scrace

Evans

It won't take us long in the van. Everybody travels so fast nowadays. When I was young a trip to the seaside took us the whole day.

5

Were there cars when you were young, Great-grandpa?

Yes, but not many people had cars. They were very slow. To start the engine you got out and turned a handle at the front.

6

Cars didn't have roofs then, so when it rained you put the hood up.

CX·318

Most roads weren't covered with smooth black tar like they are now.

They were very bumpy and in summer they were very dusty, too.

Didn't the dust get all over you?

8

Yes it did! We had to wear goggles to keep the dust out of our eyes.

10

In those days most shops would deliver the shopping. You told them what you wanted and a boy from the shop would come on a bicycle with your shopping.

11

Yes, I did, but it was very different from yours. All bikes were black then. They didn't have any gears and some didn't even have brakes!

Cycling was uncomfortable then. The streets were made of cobblestones and they were very bumpy. You had to be very careful not to get your wheels caught in the tramlines, too.

What were tramlines?

I will tell you.

15

Tramlines were like railway lines except that they were laid in the road. Trams would run along them.

What is a tram?

16

A tram was like a bus, but it ran along tramlines. The driver had a bell which he rang to tell you to get out of the way.

Before cars, people often travelled by tram or bus. Some cities still have trams to get people to work.

17

I like looking at horses. They remind me of the old days. They used to do lots of the work that cars and lorries do today.

I remember that milk was delivered to our house every day in a cart pulled by a horse. The sound of its hooves on the road used to wake me up each morning.

Like an alarm clock!

19

Horses did lots of other things, too. Before there were taxis we had hansom cabs pulled by horses to take you to where you wanted to go.

Wasn't it hard work for the horses?

They are very strong animals. One kind of horse is so strong that it was used on farms before there were tractors. It used to pull the plough and heavy farm wagons.

Does anyone know what that horse was called?

A shire horse.

How did you get to places a long way away then?

We always went by train. Trains burned coal for fuel in those days, so there was lots of smoke and steam puffing out of the engine. They were very noisy, too.

22

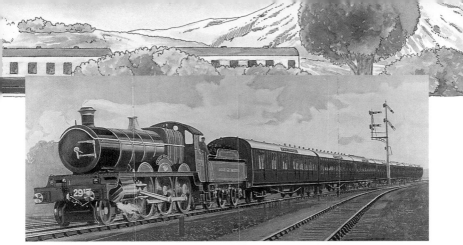

Once the engine driver let me ride in his cab. That was really exciting!

How did you get to places across the sea, Great-grandpa?

We went in big ships. They worked by steam, too, like the trains. I went for a ride on a steamer when I was a child.

There were still some sailing ships when I was young, too. They used the wind to carry them along.

25

I had only seen one or two aeroplanes when I was your age. Aeroplanes had only just been invented.

They were very small and slow. There was no room for passengers either.

28

Yes, it's nice to get quickly from place to place, but journeys were fun in the old days, too.

This page shows lots of old forms of transport. Can you remember them all?

1. Tram 2. Steamer 3. Steam train 4. Sailing ship